Me Mum Sez...

Outrageous Truths
about
Life and People

By Meg Salty

ASPEN WEST

Typesetting and Layout by R. K. & C. M. Kilcrease.
Cover Design by Ernie Harker.

Aspen West Publishing Co., Inc.
P.O. Box 1245
Sandy, Utah 84070

ISBN: 0-9615390-9-7

Printed in the United States of America

TO ALL THE MUM'S

Who vault out of bed each morning
with new bits of wisdom
for all of us.

The True Source Of All The Love, Wit And Wisdom That Guides Our Lives!

We were standing in line waiting to check through customs at the great London Gatwick airport. The agent nodded and our young daughter stepped forward and showed the agent her passport. The agent opened it and studied the contents. Then she asked, in a distinct British accent, "How long will you be staying in England?" Not being sure of the exact length of time, our daughter turned and asked us. The agent continued, "Where will you be staying?" Once again, our daughter turned and looked toward her mother for the answer. Almost as quickly, the agent inquired, "Is that yu Mum? I always ask Me Mum when I don't know something."

It didn't take us long to discover that what Me Mum Sez is held in high esteem in the British Isles, and that Me Mum had much to say about daily living on the North American Continent as well. In response to a question about the effectiveness of the British government, Me Mum Sez, "Whenever the British Parliament or the US Congress takes action on something, that is the best sign that the crises has already passed." Concerning Shakespeare's Hamlet, who said, "To be or not to be," Me Mum Sez, "Don't ask stupid questions!"

Our mothers are with us through time and maternity. We owe them our unabashed love for what they've told us when we didn't know the answer or were too scared to ask. As you will see, these mumisms joyfully support Sinclair Lewis' observation that, "There are two insults no human being will endure: that he has no sense of humor and that he has never known trouble." Although Mums know trouble, they know it with humor.

This pocket oracle brings together a wide variety of knowledge and experience, thoroughly scrutinized by Me Mum, and gives new meaning and more than a few laughs to our lives. No amount of expertise can substitute for the intimate knowledge of our Mums. So, when Me Mum Sez it, we better listen up!

Table of Contents

Table of Contents con't.

Chapter 1

Secret Mutterings to Help You Get Out of Bed in the Morning

Me Mum Sez that there are days when as soon as you open your eyes you know you are in over your head.

Philosophers say, "The early bird gets the worm,

but Me Mum Sez, "let 'em have it."

Me Mum Sez that if at first you do succeed, consider yourself among the suprised.

———————— • ————————

Henry Lorayne says that most problems precisely defined are already partially solved, but **Me Mum Sez** that that's like learning that your girlfriend plans to wear a swimming suit to the junior prom.

Me Mum Sez show me a man with two feet planted firmly on the ground and I'll show you a man who can't get his pants on.

Me Mum Sez as soon as you discover that you can just about do something, you are given something else to do.

Me Mum Sez that people who set goals miss the fun side trips.

Me Mum Sez that the sky is not the limit; it's what you decide to do right now that limits you.

Robert Louis Stevenson says
that you cannot run away from
weakness; you must sometime
fight it out or perish, but
Me Mum Sez that the ability
to lift 500 pounds has little
advantage in a feather pillow
factory.

Me Mum Sez that some people like to live the golden rule;
but real movers kick down doors, break butt,
and go for the gold.

❧10❧

Chapter 2

The Real Road to Success
is Filled With Potholes

Someone said that nice guys finish last, but Me Mum Sez that is true only if they start late.

Me Mum Sez that we should try to live someplace between the newly weds and the nearly deads.

———————— • ————————

An Adage says that hard work never hurt anyone, but Me Mum Sez not to take any unnecessary chances.

After being informed that it was 110 degrees in the shade, Me Mum Sez that she's glad we don't have to work in the shade.

———————— • ————————

Some say it doesn't matter if you win or lose, it's how you play the game; but Me Mum Sez that you better win three out of four times or there isn't going to be a game to play.

———————— • ————————

Me Mum Sez as soon as you are positive something can't be done, someone else does it well.

Me Mum Sez that keeping up with the Joneses is only
important if you are in the same race.

Me Mum Sez that you should remove the packing material before you turn on your brain.

Me Mum Sez the further you fall the higher you bounce.

Chapter 3

Breaking the Work Habit

Me Mum Sez that if you start at the bottom, you may be working your bottom off for a long time.

Me Mum Sez that you should look good, dress well, marry rich, and you won't need to look for work.

Me Mum Sez that Carl Wood is probably right when he says that the person who knows how will always have a job, and the person who knows why will be her boss.

Me Mum Sez that the only ones who know the secret to success are the ones who have not succeeded.

Me Mum Sez that retirement at 65 is ridiculous since you've already worked most of your life.

Someone said that he's bothered because he may not be working as hard as he can, but **Me Mum Sez** that it would be more scary to think that he is.

———————————— • ————————————

Me Mum Sez that it is impossible to enjoy work if there is plenty of idling to do.

Bill Cosby says that there's no labor a man can do that's undignified, if he does it right;

but Me Mum Sez here's a man who has never shoveled manure into the wind.

Me Mum Sez the customer is always right, misinformed, bullheaded, fickle, ignorant, and abominably stupid...

...but never wrong.

Chapter 4

Nightmares of Daily Living

Me Mum Sez that roses are red and violets are blue, but if there's a hog around then they'll all smell the same.

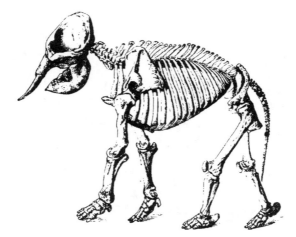

Me Mum Sez that skeketons in family closets cut down
on the storage space.

Me Mum Sez that doctors have given up on keeping people healthy and are now asking what sickness you prefer to live with.

———————— • ————————

Henry David Thoreau says that when a dog runs at you, whistle for him; but Me Mum Sez dogs don't need any musical accompaniment when they are attacking you.

Me Mum Sez that God
loves you, but everyone
else thinks you're an idiot.

Me Mum Sez that Fred Allen was right when he said that you only live once, and if you work it right once is enough.

Me Mum Sez treat a visitor as a guest for two days but on the third day give her a hoe.

———————— • ————————

Karen Elizabeth Gordon says that great men are not always idiots, but Me Mum Sez that some of our best known idiots are viewed as great men.

Me Mum Sez

that if it's good enough for
queenie,
it's good enough for her.

Me Mum Sez to get back on your feet,

you should quit standing on your head so much.

Me Mum Sez to lineup alphabetically according to height.

Chapter 5

Money **Can** get You Pretty Close To Happiness

Me Mum Sez that one doesn't possess great wealth; it possesses you.

———————— • ————————

Some sage said that money can't buy happiness, but Me Mum Sez that it can get you pretty close if you know where to shop.

Someone said that you can fool part of the people part of the time but not all of the people all of the time, but **Me Mum Sez** then why are we all paying taxes?

——————— • ———————

Me Mum Sez that little boys who tell lies get into amusement parks cheaper.

Me Mum Sez that if you want to read about going into business and make a profit, you have to read two separate books.

Me Mum Sez that optimists are people who have money in the bank when they die.

Some people spend their life saving money, but Me Mum Sez that it would be better for them to save their life and spend their money.

Benjamin Franklin averred that a penny saved is a penny earned but Me Mum Sez that if you save your pennies for a year, you will be surprised at how little you've earned in a year.

Me Mum Sez that now is the time to be frugal at all costs.

Ralph Waldo Emerson says that nothing great was ever achieved without enthusiasm, but **Me Mum Sez** that nothing great was ever achieved without proper financing and a good marketing plan.

Chapter 6

Don't Panic...Yet

Me Mum Sez to take action now and explain later.

When someone says to have a nice day, Me Mum Sez, sorry, but I'm not going to change my plans again.

———————— • ————————

Me Mum Sez that it's quite a bit easier leading friends than leading enemies.

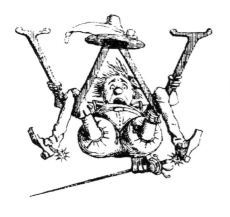

Me Mum Sez that people will only forgive your good advice if they ask for it.

Ludwig von Mises said that action is preceded by thinking, but
Me Mum Sez that the order of things is Ready, Fire, Aim!

Me Mum Sez she agrees with the idea that a mistake proves that someone stopped long enough to do something.

———————— • ————————

Me Mum Sez that whoever said it is easier to get forgiveness than permission has never tried to move fly paper.

———————— • ————————

Me Mum Sez that anybody who thinks there aren't two sides to every argument is probably in one.

Chapter 7

Marriage is a Shaky Foundation for Quality Relationships

Some people say that marriage is a 50-50 proposition,

but Me Mum Sez it's 97-3 when diapers are concerned.

Me Mum Sez that the most important thing in a relationship between a man and a woman is that they are.

Me Mum Sez that you should live in such a way that a nationally televised interview with you would not embarrass your mother-in-law.

Me Mum Sez that she believes in love at first sight, but she intends to keep practicing until she gets it right.

The latest research shows that about one - third of the men and women cheat on each other in America, but **Me Mum Sez** that the rest cheat outside the U.S.

Me Mum Sez that life is so short that we shouldn't spend so much time beating up on one another.

Aristotle Onassis says that if women didn't exist, all the money in the world would have no meaning, but Me Mum Sez that if women didn't exist, the world would have no meaning.

Chapter 8

Ex-purts are Little Drips

Me Mum Sez that people who go to psychiatrists are paying for not being interrupted, and never have so many people been paid so much for doing so little.

Will Rogers says that he never met a man he didn't like,

but Me Mum Sez that she never met a little kid that she did like.

Me Mum Sez that university professors have a lot in common with the Forest Lawn Cemetery.

Mark Twain says that against the assault of laughter nothing
can stand, but Me Mum Sez that accountants
seem more resistant than most.

~ 75 ~

Me Mum Sez that journalism consists of making mountains out of molehills for people who can't do it themselves.

Chapter 9

More Bad Advice From the Rich and the Famous

Guy Bellamy says
that hindsight is
an exact science,
but Me Mum Sez
that exact sciences
are what produced
bottles with tops
too small to fill and
bottoms too large
to pour.

Kahlil Gibran says that Nirvana comes from leading your sheep to a green pasture, and in putting your child to sleep, and in writing the last line of your poem, but Me Mum Sez that hitting a home run off of the frist pitch of the game is also quite satisfying.

Oliver Wendell Holmes says that a man's mind, stretched by a new idea, can never go back to its original dimension, but Me Mum Sez that she knows a lot of people with warped minds who are not hard to be around.

Hamlet says, To be or not to be

but Me Mum Sez, don't ask stupid questions.

~:83:~

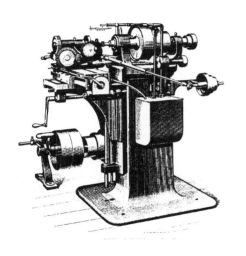

Henri Arnold says that the wise person questions himself, while the fool questions others, but **Me Mum Sez** to measure twice, cut once, and don't worry about what others think unless you are in politics.

Chapter 10

Five Second Self-Therapy

Sid Ascher says that the surest way to lose a friend is to tell him something for his own good, but Me Mum Sez that the surest way to lose a friend is to borrow her car and have an accident.

———————— • ————————

Me Mum Sez that you shouldn't jump to conclusions because you may break an ankle, but that's the only exercise some people get.

Me Mum Sez that people who can laugh
at themselves will always be amused.

Me Mum Sez that being a deeply superficial person means that you must dig down deep to find out how shallow you are.

Me Mum Sez that three things are hard to hide: love, smoke, and a person riding a camel.

———————————— • ————————————

Me Mum Sez that early to bed and early to rise is a good idea because if you get a reputation as an early riser you can sleep till noon.

Me Mum Sez that she learned the same thing about eating fruit that Adam and Eve did, that stupidity won't kill you but it can make you sweat.

———————— • ————————

Me Mum Sez that the easiest way to do anything is wrong.

Me Mum Sez that if you don't cry once in a while,

you will have to figure out another way to flush out
all the little water ducts in your body.

Me Mum Sez that with the passing of time, everything difficult becomes the good old days.

Chapter 11

What Little Kids Should Know

Me Mum Sez, always wear clean underwear; you may get in an accident.

———————————— • ————————————

Me Mum Sez, don't buy a BB gun cause you'll shoot yourself in the eye.

Someone asked,
"What is a vacation
without children?"
Me Mum Sez that
it's one that's peaceful
and paid for.

Me Mum Sez that
she and her kids have
a deal: she doesn't try
to understand them
and they don't try to
understand her.

Me Mum Sez that mothers know it all; they have eyes in the back of their heads.

————————— • —————————

Someone said that he who hesitates is lost, but Me Mum Sez to look before you leap and to expect interruptions.

————————— • —————————

Me Mum Sez that in the early days, the larger the farm, the more children a family needed. Can you hear the farmer's wife when he announces acquiring an additional 20 acres of land?

Me Mum Sez, if you pout,
a bird will poop on your lip.

A Welsh proverb says that perfect love sometimes does not come 'till the first grand-child, but Me Mum Sez that broken saucers and warts come at about the same time.

Chapter 12

Short Term Religious Living

The Good Book says that lies are an abomination to the Lord, but **Me Mum Sez** that the short term benefits are worth considering.

———————— • ————————

The Good Book says that we are all born equal, but **Me Mum Sez** that we should try to grow out of it a soon as possible.

Me Mum Sez that everyone should believe in something...

...so I believe I'll have a beer.

The Pastor says praying is talking to God, but Me Mum Sez that if God answers back regularly, it's called schizophrenia.

———————— • ————————

Me Mum Sez that we should trust in the Lord, but shouldn't go out alone after dark.

———————— • ————————

Willis Whitney says that people fight over what they do not know, but Me Mum Sez that Baptists are right and Methodists are wrong and so we go on to the end of the song.

Me Mum Sez that the good Lord never gives you more than you can handle, unless you get hit by a truck.

Me Mum Sez that I never
did give anybody hell...

...they mostly served themselves.

Me Mum Sez that God made us
with two ears that stay open and
one mouth that shuts, but we
usually do just the reverse.

Me Mum Sez that people who get in trouble usually get there by themselves.

Chapter 13

Avoiding Personal Productivity

Me Mum Sez that nothing makes a person more
productive than the last minute.

Moses Maimonides said to teach thy tongue to say I know not, and then thou wilt progress, but Me Mum Sez to put your foot in the middle of a person's back and progress comes much faster.

———————— • ————————

Sandy Cooley says that the best cure for insomnia is Monday morning, but Me Mum Sez that evidence of the resurrection comes every Friday at about 5:00 PM when there is a great awakening.

Me Mum Sez that when you are up to your butt in alligators,

don't spend time swatting the mosquitos.

Me Mum Sez that every time you aim nowhere you always get there.

F. Scott Fitzgerald says that vitality shows not only in the ability to persist but in the ability to start over, but **Me Mum Sez** that if you get it right the first time, you'll have more time to play.

Me Mum Sez that you should never look back or you'll rear-end the car in front of you.

———— • ————

A familiar rural adage says that a kick in the rear is a step forward, but Me Mum Sez that a 2x4-side-the-head is more effective.

Will Rogers said that even if you're on the right track, you'll get run over if you just sit there, but Me Mum Sez that it depends on the time of day.

Chapter 14

Keeping Friends at a Safe Distance

Me Mum Sez that people who think they are the best at everything are always bothersome to us who are.

———————— • ————————

Me Mum Sez that a coward dies a thousand deaths, thus it is easier to be brave when there is no danger.

Me Mum Sez that a critic is a person who knows how to do everything but can't do anything.

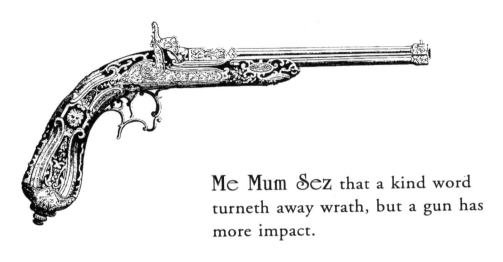

Me Mum Sez that a kind word turneth away wrath, but a gun has more impact.

Me Mum Sez that a person without character is not only dull, but the cause of dullness in others.

Me Mum Sez she had
a friend who was smarter
than a tree full of owls.

Chapter 15

How to Ambush a Politician

Elbert Hubbard says that everyone is a damn fool for at least five minutes every day, but **Me Mum Sez** that too many politicians exceed the time limit.

Me Mum Sez that, like Slick Willie, Big Al wants to print Madonna's photograph on stamps to erase the national debt.

————— • —————

Me Mum Sez that the current presidential candidates have such little talent that they would lose if they ran unopposed.

Me Mum Sez that she visited Washington D.C. and never met a politician who was carrying a full load of bricks.

Me Mum Sez that most
politicians should have
pacemakers installed
in their brains.

Me Mum Sez that the Soviet leader, Krushchev, expressed her feelings about political conventions when he said, "It is enough to make a stone sad."

———————— • ————————

After hearing about Saddam Hussein's illness, Me Mum Sez that we should all pray that it's not too trivial.

Me Mum Sez that hell for a senator is having a speech recorded that will never be heard or read by anyone.

Me Mum Sez that whenever the British Parliament or the US Congress takes action on something, that is the best sign that the crisis has already passed.

Me Mum Sez that nowadays
some politicians can
read and write.

Me Mum Sez that you have to be careful that you don't quote politicians accurately or you'll be charged with mudslinging.

———————— • ————————

Me Mum Sez that if you are going to be cremated, request that at least 30 percent of the ashes be thrown in your congressman's face.

Me Mum Sez that when a great idea and a politician's

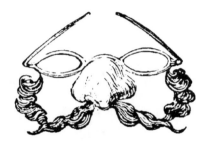

brain collide, usually nothing happens.

Me Mum Sez that there is a natural bonding between free food and politicians.

Chapter 16

*Heard any **True** Success Stories Lately?*

Me Mum Sez that the trouble with life in the fast lane is that you run out of gas sooner.

———————— • ————————

Henry David Thoreau says that we should make the most of our regrets. To regret deeply is to live afresh, but Me Mum Sez that she may have done better to take the clean wash down before the cows came through the yard.

Me Mum Sez tight shoes can help you forget all your other troubles.

Me Mum Sez that after all is said and done, something else usually happens.

Me Mum Sez that any supplies necessary for either today's events or yesterday's activities are to be ordered no later than noon tomorrow.

——————— • ———————

Most people climb the ladder of success rung by rung, but **Me Mum Sez** that elevators are a lot quicker.

Me Mum Sez that when the going gets tough,

the smart people have already gone.

Me Mum Sez that nothing ever goes away, it just gets re-organized occasionally.

Bertrand Russell says that to be without some of the things you want is an indispensable part of happiness, but Me Mum Sez that a feather tick beats sleeping on the boards.

———————— • ————————

The art of getting things done is noble, but Me Mum Sez that the grandest part of all is knowing what things to leave undone.

Me Mum Sez that crime in the streets wouldn't bother anyone if they stayed on the sidewalks.

Me Mum Sez that good advice usually works best when preceded by a whack to the side of the head.

Edith Sitwell says that we should be ourselves, if one is a greyhound why try to look like a Pekingese...

...but Me Mum Sez the best argument for make-up is a good mirror.

Me Mum Sez that most people make the mistake of trying to be themselves.

Me Mum Sez you shouldn't hold a grudge, even against people who have done things you'll never forgive.

——————— • ———————

Bill Copeland says that we should try to be like the turtle, at ease in your own shell; but **Me Mum Sez** that's the same way they cook lobsters, in their own shell.

Dorothy Parker says that she
could do without four things:
love, curiosity, freckles, and
doubt; but Me Mum Sez
she left out bow legs.

Me Mum Sez it's good to be brave, intelligent, loyal, resourceful, and sneaky.

Me Mum Sez
that schizophrenia
beats living alone.

Me Mum Sez that inverse paranoids
are her favorite people because they
are out to do everybody good.

Chapter 17

Zig-Zag Thinking

A common proverb says
that early to bed and early
to rise makes a person
healthy, wealthy, and wise,
but Me Mum Sez that
you miss all the good movies
and end up fixing your own
breakfast that way.

The old adage says that one should eat, drink, and be merry, for tomorrow we may die, but **Me Mum Sez** that it will probably be a lot longer than that.

Me Mum Sez the only real constant is change, sometimes.

———————— • ————————

Don't trust anyone! Me Mum Sez, Who said that?

———————— • ————————

Me Mum Sez if it's not where it ought to be, then it's some place else.

Me Mum Sez that if you see food arranged artistically on your plate, you know someone has been there before you.

Someone asked what she thought of Democracy in America, and Me Mum Sez she thinks it would be a good idea.

Me Mum Sez to her multi-personality friend, are you the person to whom I'm speaking.

Me Mum Sez that if you start the day by getting out of bed, you will usually have to fix someone's breakfast.

•

Me Mum Sez that you shouldn't say I guess I'll leave, since you can only leave or not leave; you can't guess you'll leave.

Chapter 18

Wise Adages Ignore the Truth

Montaigne says that the pleasantest things in life are pleasant thoughts, but **Me Mum Sez**, that a shrimp salad and a chocolate mousse once in a while aren't too bad either.

Walt Kelly says that when "I don't have anything to worry about, I begin to worry about that," but **Me Mum Sez** not to worry about anything that looks in better health or is younger than you and doesn't have whiskers.

Some people say that the difference between a good haircut and a bad one is the barber, but Me Mum Sez it's about a week.

You can't lose weight by talking about it--you have to keep your mouth shut, but Me Mum Sez that bragging about it is half the fun.

When someone says that life begins at forty, Me Mum Sez that's true only if the kids are gone, the relatives leave, and the dog dies.

Chapter 19

Famous Cities,
Until You Have Been There

Poets say to breathe deeply the elixir of life, but Me Mum Sez that if you make a sudden move like that in Chicago, you'll end up in a morgue.

Me Mum Sez if I had a farm in Kansas and a home in hell, I'd sell my farm and move home.

Me Mum Sez have you ever noticed how many people

in Hollywood put masks over their masks?

Me Mum Sez that in San Francisco, some people celebrate Halloween every night.

———————— • ————————

Me Mum Sez I just received this note from Helen Hunt. If you lost your wallet recently, you'll have to go to Helen Hunt for it.

Me Mum Sez that Chicken
Little would never make it
in New York.

Me Mum Sez that the wages of sin have steadily increased in downtown L.A.

Me Mum Sez that the best view of your old neighborhood is through the rear view mirror.

Chapter 20

Worldwide Starvation From People
Writing Food for Thought

H.L. Mencken says that there are two kinds of books; those that no one reads and those that no one ought to read, but Me Mum Sez that those that no one reads or ought to read are one kind; the other kind are behind the counter.

———— • ————

Wentworth Dillon says to choose an author as you choose a friend, but Me Mum Sez it would be better if we could choose our relatives like we check books out of the library.

Me Mum Sez that many great best sellers probably could have been prevented by their college English teachers.

Me Mum Sez that the reason why so few good books are read is because they are not published yet.

———————— • ————————

Me Mum Sez that community values are reflected in newspaper headlines such as, "Major California Earth Quake Nearly Destroys Football Stadium".

Me Mum Sez that the newspaper comics are for people who can't read, editorials are for people who can't think, and the sports pages are for people who can't sit around doing nothing.

Me Mum Sez that there is so much garbage being produced today that if it weren't for TV there'd be no place to put it all.

———————— • ————————

Thomas Siler says that oratory leaves a smoke screen; eloquence, a vapor trail; sincerity, an endowment, but Me Mum Sez that poison oak leaves a rash.

END OF THE VOLUME.

Dear Bunky (All of Me Mum's readers),

If yur Mum has said sumthin' you'd like to share with the world, please jot it down on a scrap of paper and shoot if off to us. We'll try to include it in a future volume of <u>Me Mum Sez</u>. Oh, include your address so we can get back to you.

With Love,

Meg Salty

p.s. If we use your Mum's saying, we'll send you a free copy of a new
      edition of <u>Me Mum Sez</u>.

**Please ask your local retail Gift or Bookstore
about other fine products**

ASPEN WEST
PUBLISHING & DISRIBUTION

9615390-9-7 Me Mum Sez... $5.95
9615390-0-3 "Where's Mom Now That I Need Her?"
                 (H.B.)Surviving Away From Home.. $21.95
9615390-1-1 "Where's Mom..." (Paperback)... $12.95
9615390-2-X "Where's Dad Now That I Need Him?"
                 (H.B.)Surviving Away From Home.. $21.95
9615390-3-8 "Where's Dad..." (Paperback).. $12.95

Free catalog upon request.
Please add $2.50 per book for shipping and handling.

Aspen West Publishing Co. Inc. , P.O. Box 1245, Sandy, Utah 84070
801-565-1370 • 800-222-9133 • FAX 801-565-1373